A CENTENNIAL CHECK-LIST
OF THE EDITIONS OF
HENRY DAVID THOREAU'S
Walden

BY

WALTER HARDING

THE UNIVERSITY OF VIRGINIA PRESS

FOR THE

BIBLIOGRAPHICAL SOCIETY
OF THE UNIVERSITY OF VIRGINIA
CHARLOTTESVILLE, VIRGINIA, 1954

TO

MRS. CALEB WHEELER

TO WHOM ALL MODERN THOREAU
SCHOLARS ARE INDEBTED FOR
HER FRIENDLY ASSISTANCE AND
FOR HER VAST KNOWLEDGE OF
NINETEENTH-CENTURY CONCORD

ACKNOWLEDGMENTS

I have been exceedingly fortunate in obtaining the aid of many Thoreau collectors and librarians in the compilation of this check-list——far too many, in fact, for me to attempt to list their names in full. But I wish to express my particular thanks to Mr. Francis H. Allen, Blackie & Son, Ltd., Mr. John Cooley, Mr. William Cummings, Mr. T. Y. Davis, Mr. Harvey Deal, Mr. Francis Dedmond (for particular help with foreign editions), Mr. Anton Kovar, Mr. A. E. Lownes, Mrs. Helen Morrison, Mr. F. M. Oliver, Mr. Leo Shapiro, Mr. R. M. Sills, Mr. Arthur Volkman, and Dr. Viola White (for information about editions in the Abernethy Library of Middlebury College). I am also indebted to the many members of the Thoreau Society who replied to my queries in the *Thoreau Society Bulletin* (where I printed a preliminary check-list in the issue of Spring, 1952) and to the library staffs of the University of Virginia, Princeton University, and the Library of Congress.

Preface

THE growth of interest in Thoreau's *Walden* over the century since its publication is a major phenomenon in the annals of American literature. It took eight years to sell the first impression of two thousand copies. Yet now it can perhaps rightfully be claimed that it has since been more frequently reprinted than any other book-length work in American literature written before the Civil War. It seems fitting therefore, as we approach the centennial of its publication, to issue this check-list of the known editions of *Walden* to help chart the curve of its rise in popularity and to show its spread of appeal from New England to the four corners of the earth.

The nucleus of this check-list was formed from my own personal collection of editions of *Walden*. But it has been supplemented with information derived from all the bibliographies of Thoreau, the standard bibliographical reference guides in the University of Virginia Library, book catalogs, and various collections of Thoreauviana.

The editions are listed and numbered chronologically. Where more than one edition appeared in any one year, they are listed alphabetically by publisher. Sub-editions (that is, use of the same plates by different publishers or by the same publisher under a different "edition name") are listed as separate editions but with an indication of the parent edition. Varying impressions are discussed only with the first edition. I have tried to include in this check-list all regular editions of *Walden*, all foreign translations, all digests, and all separate printings of portions of *Walden*. I have not included excerpts from the book included in anthologies.

I have tried to keep bibliographical details to a minimum but to give sufficient information to distinguish the individual editions. I have not listed the title unless it varied from *Walden* or *Walden, or Life in the Woods*, or a reasonably close foreign translation thereof. With the exception again of the first edition, I have made no attempt to describe bindings, although occasionally I have noted that variant bindings occur. Neither have I attempted to describe variant illustrations, although where I have discovered their existence, I have so noted.

Unfortunately I have been unable to locate for examination every single edition listed herein. Therefore it is quite possible that in a few cases sub-editions have not been identified as such, and occasionally I have been unable to supply full bibliographical information. I have indicated with an asterisk (*) all those editions which I have examined personally.

It is my hope that this check-list will not only serve as a guide to collectors of Thoreauviana, but also that it may serve to trace the widening influence of Thoreau.

Charlottesville, Virginia

February 3, 1953

Check-List

1.   1854. Boston: Ticknor and Fields. 357 p.

*The first impression: Two thousand copies of the first impression (what collectors and dealers often loosely call the first edition) were printed, and the book was put on sale in August, 1854.

This is the only impression from these plates to carry the sub-title "or, Life in the Woods" on the titlepage. In an unpublished letter (the manuscript of which is now in the Huntington Library, San Marino, Calif.) to Messrs. Ticknor & Fields of March 4, 1862, just two months before his death, Thoreau wrote requesting that the sub-title be dropped on all future editions (*i. e.*, impressions).

Collectors and dealers have built up a tradition of "points" based on some variant features not conjugate with the text. It has thus seemed wise to deal with these briefly: one popular "point" with the first impression is the dating of the advertisements at the end of the volume. A premium price is usually demanded for advertisements dated "April, 1854," although the book was not published until four months later. It is the opinion of most students of printing that the first copies off the press would have been more likely to include either August or September advertisements, the printer reverting to the earlier advertising pages when his current supply was used up. Actually the dating of the advertisements has little meaning, for it was the habit of publishers to run off a large impression at once and then bind the sheets as copies were needed on the market, inserting whatever advertisements were on hand at the moment. The earliest advertisements I have discovered are April, 1854 (fairly common), and the latest September, 1855 (a copy in the library of Mr. Albert E. Lownes of Providence, R. I.).

Aside from the advertisements, the only other bibliographical point in the first impression is the engraved map of Walden Pond which in some copies faces page 306, in others page 307, and in still others is omitted entirely. Mr.

Lownes owns two copies with June, 1854, advertisements but with the map facing different pages, so this seems to offer no conclusive evidence for dating individual copies. The omission of the map in some copies is perhaps explained by an entry in the Ticknor and Fields Cost Books indicating that 500 extra maps were ordered in Sept. 1856. Apparently some of the first order of maps were damaged and destroyed, and when the supply on hand was exhausted, at least a few copies were bound up before the new order of maps was filled.

The binding of the first impression varies slightly. Most copies are in olive drab cloth, but occasionally some are bound in a somewhat redder brown. But again, since all the sheets were printed at once and then bound individually as they were needed, there is no great significance to the color of the binding. The endpapers of all copies of the first impression that I have seen are lemon yellow.

*The second impression: A second impression of 280 copies was made in March and April of 1862 and released a few weeks after Thoreau's death on May 6, 1862. Strangely enough the existence of this second and of the third impressions was not known to collectors until it was pointed out by Prof. Raymond Adams in an article in *American Literature*, II (May, 1930), 166-168, entitled "A Bibliographical Note on *Walden*." This was confirmed by the publication of the Ticknor and Field Cost Books by W. S. Tryon and William Charvat (New York: Bibliographical Society of America, 1949, p. 289-290). The binding of this impression is unchanged, but the endpapers are chocolate brown.

The third impression: A third impression of 280 copies was made in November and December, 1862, but all are apparently dated 1863. With the exception of the dating they are like the second impression.

The fourth impression: This was long erroneously called the "second edition." It was issued in 1864, and except for the date is like the second and third impressions.

*Later impressions: The stereotype plates for the first edition were used by Ticknor & Fields and its various successors at least as late as 1885, when an impression labeled on the titlepage "Twenty-third Edition" was issued, and probably up until 1889 when new plates for the Riverside Aldine Edition were made. By this time many of the plates had been damaged and some repaired. These repairs are easily noted in the later impressions through the occasional occurrence of letters, words, and phrases in a darker type, as for example the letters "re" in the word "furniture" in the 24th line on page 71.

One curious bibliographical idiosyncracy is the phrase "The End" on page 357. In some impressions of the first edition it occurs with a period, in some without, and in some the whole phrase is omitted. Normally one would expect a gradual deterioration of the plate, with the period breaking off first and then the whole phrase becoming so broken that it would be chiseled off the plate. But I have found a copy of the 1862 impression which omits the period and one of the impression of 1876 which includes it. This could occur either through the occasional mixing of sheets from different impressions or through the phrase being set up separately from the plate for the page.

In his "Thoreau Newsletter" for October, 1944 (Chapel Hill, mimeographed), Prof. Adams points out:

> In 1865 began what we might call the "Oak Leaf Edition" of WALDEN, though I cannot yet be sure whether the leaves on the backstrip are oak or holly. Anyway, the bindings are more ornate, with gilt rustic work on the backstrips. Thoreau's initials appear over his name, and he is called "Author of EXCURSIONS and A WEEK ON CONCORD RIVER." In 1865 the cloth is heavily pebbled in regular rows, is black, and has ivy leaves blind-stamped at the corners of the covers. In 1866 the pebbling is random, the color is chocolate brown, and the blind-stamp is a wreath in the center of the covers. In 1873 the pebbling has disappeared and the cloth is black, but the stamping remains the same. So in 1875, by which time the book has achieved fatness, being 3/16th of an inch thicker than two years before. And so I come to the 1881 edition, the same plates now badly broken, but in a new format. The page size is 7 1/2 x 5 inches as compared with 7 x 4 1/2 in 1875.

The binding is smooth, dark green cloth over heavy boards, the backstrip is stamped "WALDEN / THOREAU / Houghton Mifflin & Co." and the signature "Henry D. Thoreau" is stamped in gilt on the front cover. The map of the pond disappeared from the book after 1865. Between 1878 and 1881 Thoreau's books were being issued in a bright "oak leaf" binding that might be called reddish-brown. I have copies in this binding of everything except WALDEN. Was there a reddish-brown WALDEN, I wonder?

I have been unable to answer Prof. Adams' final question, but I might add that the 1881 binding was still used as late as 1885 and that the edges were beveled. It should also be added that all sorts of variations from Prof. Adams' schedule of bindings will be found due both to the publisher's practice, already mentioned, of binding in small lots and to the possibility of mixing sheets from various impressions. For example, I have a copy of the 1862 impression with the 1866 binding, and many other such variations will be found. Parent edition of 2.

2. 1884. London: Hamilton, Adams & Co. and Edinburgh: David Douglas. 357 p.

This is apparently the American edition with a new titlepage. It was the first edition of *Walden* to appear under an English imprint, although apparently some copies of the 1854 impression were shipped to England in 1855 and the English publishers may have affixed a gummed sticker of their imprint to the titlepage as was a common custom, although I have seen no copies so treated. A sub-edition of 1.

3. 1886.* London: Walter Scott. xxviii, 336 p. With an introduction by Will H. Dircks.

This is the first original English edition and is a volume in the Camelot Classics. It includes in an appendix an extract from Thoreau's *Week* and three of his poems. Parent edition of 4, 7, 10, 33.

4. 1888. London: Walter Scott and Toronto: W. J. Gage & Co. xxviii, 336 p. With an introduction by Will H. Dircks. A sub-edition of 3.

5. 1889.* Boston: Houghton, Mifflin and Company. 2 vol., 514 p. Riverside Aldine Series Edition.

This is the first edition to use Thoreau's corrections and revisions of the text, although all of them have not as yet been incorporated into any edition of *Walden*. See Reginald Cook's transcript of Thoreau's annotations of *Walden, Thoreau Society Bulletin* No. 42 (Winter, 1953).

In the first chapter there is a list of foods which Thoreau used at Walden Pond (Page 95 of this edition) and along the right-hand side a bracket labeled "All experiments which failed." In the first edition this bracket did not include "Salt," the last item on the list. But the typesetter of this edition erred and extended it to include "Salt." This error, thus established, has persisted through most modern editions of the book. Parent edition of 6, 8, 9, 11, 12, 13, 15, 26, 28, 52.

6. 1889. Boston: Houghton, Mifflin and Company. 2 vol., 514 p. A limited edition of the Riverside Aldine Series Edition was issued with paper labels and uncut pages. A sub-edition of 5.

7. 1891. London: Walter Scott. xxviii, 336 p. One volume of a three volume set of the works of Thoreau. A sub-edition of 3.

8. 1893.* Boston: Houghton Mifflin Company. vi, 522 p. With an unsigned introduction and an index. Volume Two of the Riverside Edition of Thoreau's works, later labeled the New Riverside Edition. A sub-edition of 5.

9. 1893.* Boston: Houghton Mifflin Company. vi, 522 p. With an unsigned introduction and an index. The Large-Paper Edition of the Riverside Edition. Limited to 150 copies. A sub-edition of 5.

10. 1895. London: Walter Scott Limited. xxx, 336 p. With an introduction by Will H. Dircks and an electro-gravure frontispiece of Walden Pond. A sub-edition of 3.

11. 1897.* Boston: Houghton, Mifflin and Company. 2 vol., xliii, 1-259; vi, 261-522 p. With an introduction by

Bradford Torrey, photogravures chiefly by A. W. Hosmer, and an index. The Holiday Edition (although not labeled as such on the individual copies). A sub-edition of 5.

12. 1897. London: Gay & Bird. 2 vol., xliii, 1-259; vi, 261-522 p. With an introduction by Bradford Torrey, photogravures chiefly by A. Hosmer, and an index. An English Holiday Edition. A sub-edition of 5.

13. 1897. Boston: Houghton, Mifflin & Co. xxxviii, 522 p. With a biographical sketch by Ralph Waldo Emerson. The Popular Edition. A sub-edition of 5.

14. 1897. Munchen: Verlag Concord (J. Palm). xxii, 356 p. Translated into German by Emma Emmerich.

15. 1898. Boston: Houghton, Mifflin & Co. xxxviii, 522 p. With a biographical sketch by Ralph Waldo Emerson. The Cambridge Classics Edition. A sub-edition of 5.

16. 1899.* Philadelphia: Henry Altemus Company. 375 p. With a frontispiece portrait of Thoreau.

17. 1899. New York: T. Y. Crowell & Company. xvi, 350 p. With an introduction by Charles D. G. Roberts and a frontispiece portrait of Thoreau. The Faience Edition. Parent edition of 18, 19, 20, 21, 22.

18. 1899. New York: T. Y. Crowell & Company. xvi, 350 p. With an introduction by Charles D. G. Roberts. The Handy Edition. A sub-edition of 17.

19. 1899. New York: T. Y. Crowell & Company. xvi, 350 p. With an introduction by Charles D. G. Roberts. The Limp Leather Edition. A sub-edition of 17.

20. 1899.* New York: T. Y. Crowell & Company. xvi, 350 p. With an introduction by Charles D. G. Roberts. The Oak Leaf Edition. A sub-edition of 17.

21. 1899. New York: T. Y. Crowell & Company. xvi, 350 p. With an introduction by Charles D. G. Roberts. The Ruskin Edition. A sub-edition of 17.

22.   1899. New York: T. Y. Crowell & Company. xvi, 350 p. With an introduction by Charles D. G. Roberts. The Waldorf Edition. A sub-edition of 17.

23.   1900?* New York: A. L. Burt Company. 373 p. With a frontispiece drawing of Thoreau hoeing beans. Home Library Edition.

This edition is undated in all the copies I have seen. The lack of copyright date would seem to imply publication after 1910 when the copyright expired. But I have seen advertisements for it as early as 1902. And Mrs. Helen Morrison of Oberlin, Ohio, has written me of a copy which she states her mother purchased in 1900. Parent edition of 24, 25.

24.   1902? New York: A. L. Burt Company. 373 p. The Cornell Series Edition. A sub-edition of 23.

25.   1902? New York: A. L. Burt Company. 373 p. New Pocket Edition. I have assumed the simultaneous publication of this edition with that of 23 and 24, since they are identical except for binding. But the earliest advertisements I have been able to discover for this edition are in 1915, so it is possible that it was not issued until that date. A sub-edition of 23.

26.   1902. London: Gay & Bird. xliii, 522 p. With an introduction by Bradford Torrey, photogravures chiefly by A. W. Hosmer, and an index. An English New Holiday Edition. A sub-edition of 5.

27.   1902.* Bussum, Netherlands: C. J. W. Grentzebach. iii, 379 p. Translated into Dutch by Suze de Jongh van Damwoude. With a foreword by Frederik Van Eeden and an introduction by Will H. Dircks.

This edition was a product of a little socialist community outside Amsterdam, the story of which is told by C. W. Bieling in *Thoreau Society Bulletin* No. 14 (January, 1946), which also includes an English translation of Van Eeden's foreword. The cloth-bound copies of this edition contain endpapers hand-blocked at the Walden community.

28. 1902. Boston: Houghton Mifflin & Company. xliii, 522 p. With an introduction by Bradford Torrey, photogravures chiefly by A. W. Hosmer, and an index. The New Holiday Edition. A sub-edition of 5.

29. 1904. New York: E. P. Dutton & Co. 256 p. With an introduction by Ralph Waldo Emerson. A sub-edition of 31.

30. 1904.* London: Arthur C. Fifield (Simple Life Press). 158 p. Varying illustrations. An abridged edition.

Thoreau was a particular favorite of the early leaders of the British Labour Party, so much so that some of their local groups were known as "Walden Clubs." This abridged edition was issued particularly to meet their demand.

31. 1904. London: George Routledge & Sons. 256 p. With an introductory essay by Ralph Waldo Emerson. Morley's Universal Library Edition. Parent edition of 29.

32. 1905.* Jena: Eugen Diederichs. xxiii, 340 p. Translated into German. Annotated and with an introduction by Wilhelm Nobbe and a frontispiece portrait of Thoreau. This edition was re-issued in 1922.

33. 1905*. London: Walter Scott, Ltd. xxviii, 336 p. With an introduction by Will H. Dircks. Volume Three in the Scott Library. A sub-edition of 3.

34. 1906. London: Blackie and Son Ltd. xi, 410 p. With an introduction by Richard Whiteing and a frontispiece portrait of Thoreau. Red Letter Library Edition.

35. 1906.* Boston: Houghton Mifflin and Company. x, 375 p. With an unsigned introduction, index, and five photogravures from photographs by Herbert W. Gleason.

This is Volume Two of the Manuscript Edition of the Writings of Thoreau. It is printed on special paper watermarked "Thoreau" in an edition limited to six hundred copies.

In the first edition of *Walden*, in the final chapter, Thoreau speaks of addressing Bright the ox with the terms *"hush"* and *"who."* When Francis H. Allen edited this edition, he was convinced that Thoreau was in error and changed this to read *"hĩsh"* and *"whoa."* Mr. Allen has however written to me recently that he is now convinced that it was he and not Thoreau who was in error, but his change has been copied in some recent editions. Parent edition of 36, 37, 44, 53, 72, 73, 77.

36. 1906. Boston: Houghton Mifflin Company. 367 p. Photographs by Herbert W. Gleason. The Riverside Library Edition. A sub-edition of 35.

37. 1906.* Boston: Houghton, Mifflin & Co. x, 375 p. With an unsigned introduction, index, and five photogravures by Herbert W. Gleason. Volume Two of the Walden Edition of the Writings of Thoreau. A sub-edition of 35.

38. 1906.* London: Oxford University Press (Henry Frowde). xvi, 299 p. With an introduction by Theodore Watts-Dunton. The World Classics Edition.

39. 1908.* London: J. M. Dent & Co. xiii, 294 p. With an introduction by Walter Raymond. The Everyman's Library Edition. Parent edition of 40, 41.

40. 1908. New York: Dutton. xiii, 294 p. With an introduction by Walter Raymond. The Best Books Series Edition. A sub-edition of 39.

41. 1908. New York: Dutton. xiii, 294 p. With an introduction by Walter Raymond. The Everyman's Library Edition (American). A sub-edition of 39.

42. 1909.* Boston: The Bibliophile Society. 2 vol. xxxii, 208; 263 p. With prefatory remarks by Henry H. Harper, introduction by F. B. Sanborn, and photographs, engravings, and manuscript facsimiles. Edition limited to 461 copies on handmade paper, 9 on Japanese vellum, and 13 additional copies.

Discovering a manuscript of *Walden* (now in the Huntington Library in San Marino, Calif.) Sanborn theorized that the publishers had cut the volume. He then attempted to print a "complete" *Walden*. But unfortunately he also attempted to rearrange the text to suit his own notions and ended with a badly garbled version that has been the despair of all serious students ever since. Virtually the only value other than that of a literary curiosity lies in Sanborn's annotations based on his own personal acquaintance with Thoreau, but even these must be accepted only with reservations.

43.   1910.* New York: Thomas Y. Crowell Company. xi, 440 p. With an introduction and photographs by Clifton Johnson. This edition was issued in various bindings. The expiration of the copyright of *Walden* in 1910 explains the large number of new editions by various publishers in that year. Parent edition of: 45, 50, 51, 84, 123.

44.   1910.* Boston: Houghton Mifflin Company. xxv, 449 p. With introduction, notes, and index by Francis H. Allen. Riverside Literature Series edition. This is by far the best annotated edition yet produced. A sub-edition of 35.

45.   1910. New York: Kelmscott Society. 440 p. With photographs by Clifton Johnson. A sub-edition of 43.

46.   1910.* New York: Longmans, Green and Co. xx, 283 p. With an introduction and notes by Raymond MacDonald Alden and a frontispiece map of Concord and vicinity. Longmans' English Classics Edition.

47.   1910.* New York: The Macmillan Company. xxx, 388 p. With introduction and notes by Byron Rees and a frontispiece portrait of Thoreau. The Macmillan's Pocket American and English Classics Edition.

48.   1910.* New York: Charles E. Merrill Co. 437 p. With an introduction, notes, and discussion questions by J. Milnor Dorey and a frontispiece portrait of Thoreau. The Merrill's English Texts Edition.
     There is a delightful and devastating analysis of the careless annotation of this edition by Francis H. Allen in "English as She Is Edited," *Atlantic Monthly*, CXIII (March, 1914), Contributors' Column.

49.   1910. Moskva:——?—— Translated into Russian by P. A. Bulanizke. With a biographical sketch by R. W. Emerson.

50. 1911. London: George G. Harrup and Company. xvi, 440 p. With photographs by Clifton Johnson. A sub-edition of 43.

51. 1914. New York: Thomas Y. Crowell Company. 440 p. Crowell's Thin Paper Pocket Edition. A sub-edition of 43.

52. 1915.* Boston: Houghton Mifflin Company. xviii, 531 p. Volume Two of the Riverside Pocket Edition of Thoreau's works. A sub-edition of 5.

53. 1919.* Boston: Houghton Mifflin Company. x, 431 p. With introduction and notes by Francis H. Allen and sixteen photographs by H. W. Gleason and A. W. Hosmer. The Visitors' Edition. A sub-edition of 35.

54. 1917. New York: Scott, Foresman and Company. 341 p. Edited by James Cloyd Bowman. The Lake English Classics Edition. Parent edition of 59.

55. 1921. London: Macmillan and Company, Ltd. 149 p. Edited by A. Cruse. An abridged edition. Entitled *Chapters from Walden*. English Literature Series for Schools Edition.

56. 1922.*Berlin: D. Hendel. x, 310 p. Translated into German and with an introduction by F. Meyer.

There is no date in the volume, and the introduction is dated 1914, but it seems certain that it was not published until 1922.

57. 1922.* Paris: La Nouvelle Revue Française. 271 p. Translated into French by Louis Fabulet.

An amusing account of the difficulties Mr. Fabulet had with the translating will be found in Francis H. Allen's "The French Translation of *Walden*," *Thoreau Society Bulletin* No. 38 (Winter, 1952). Parent edition of 58. This was issued in an edition of 840 numbered copies, but has since been frequently reprinted.

58. 1922. Paris: La Nouvelle Revue Française. 271 p. Translated into French by Louis Fabulet. A special first edition of 108 numbered copies with slightly different title page was printed for "Bibliophiles de la Nouvelle Revue Française." A sub-edition of 57.

59. 1922. New York: Scott, Foresman and Company. 348 p. Edited by James Cloyd Bowman. The Lake English Classics Edition. "Revised edition with helps to study." A sub-edition of 54.

60. 1922. Tokyo?:——?——. 200 p. With an introduction and notes in Japanese by Kinsaku Shinoda. Parent edition of 74?

61. 1924. Prague: B. Z. Nekovarik. 273 p. Translated into Czechoslovakian. With a biographical sketch by R. W. Emerson.

62. 1924. Waltham Saint Lawrence (Berks.): Golden Cockerel Press. 46 p. A partial text. Entitled *Where I Lived and What I Lived For*. Edition limited to 350 copies for sale. Parent edition of 63.

63. 1924. New York: Chaucer Head, Inc. 45 p. A partial text. Entitled *Where I Lived and What I Lived For*. Limited edition. A sub-edition of 62.

64. 1925. Tokyo?:——?——. Translated into Japanese by Imai. Parent edition of 83?

65. 1926. Glasgow: Blackie and Son. 422 p. With an introduction by Richard Whiteing. Wallet Library Edition.

66. 1927.* London: Chapman & Hall Ltd. vii, 289 p. With an unsigned introduction and illustrated with woodcuts by Eric Fitch Daglish. Parent edition of 67, 68, 79.

67. 1927. London: Chapman & Hall Ltd. vii, 289 p. With an unsigned introduction and illustrated with woodcuts by Eric Fitch Daglish. A special edition, limited to 100 copies, issued on handmade paper, with the plates on Japanese vellum, numbered and signed by the artist. A sub-edition of 66.

68. 1927. Boston: Houghton Mifflin Company. vii, 289 p. With an unsigned introduction and illustrated with woodcuts by Eric Fitch Daglish. A sub-edition of 66.

69. 1928.* Venezia: La Nuova Italia. 461 p. Translated into Italian by Guido Ferrando.

70. 1928. Westport: Georgian Press. iv, 31 p. Entitled *Winter Animals / An Essay*. "Sixty copies printed for Esther & Richard Ellis as a Greeting to their friends."

List No. 6 of the Chiswick Bookshop (New York, 1953) describes this as "20 copies printed for Mitchell Kennerley." So there is a possibility of a sub-edition of this.

71. 1929.* New York: The Book League of America. xix, 375 p. With an introduction by Joseph L. King. "Special edition published by arrangement with The Macmillan Company." A sub-edition of 75.

72. 1929. Boston: Houghton Mifflin Company. iv, 367 p. With a frontispiece photograph of Walden Pond. Riverside Library Edition. A sub-edition of 35.

73. 1929.* Boston: Houghton Mifflin Company. iv, 367 p. Bound in with *A Week* as Volume One of the Concord Edition. A sub-edition of 35.

74. 1929. Tokyo: Kenkyusha. 200 p. With an introduction and notes by Kinsaku Shinoda. A partial text including only four chapters. Kenkyusha Pocket English Series Edition. Probably a sub-edition of 60.

75. 1929.* New York: The Macmillan Company. xix, 375 p. With an introduction by Joseph L. King. The Modern Readers' Series Edition. Parent edition of 71, 88.

76. 1930.* Chappaqua: Bibliophile Press. 4 p. A partial text. Entitled *Two Extracts from the Concluding Chapter of Walden or, Life in the Woods and My Prayer*. 100 copies printed.

77. 1930.* Boston: Houghton Mifflin Company. x, 375 p. Volume Nineteen of the Out-of-Door Library (School Edition). A sub-edition of 35.

78. 1930.* Chicago: Lakeside Press. xv, 355 p. With an introduction by Raymond Adams and illustrations by Rudolph Ruzicka. Limited to one thousand copies.

79. 1931. London: Chapman & Hall. vii, 289 p. With an unsigned introduction and illustrated with woodcuts by Eric Fitch Daglish. A sub-edition of 66.

80. 1932. Chicago: Chicago Public Library. 6 vol. Transcribed into Grade 1½ Braille from "the Houghton Mifflin 1917 edition."

81. 1933. Praze: Otto. 276 p. Translated into Czechoslovakian by Milos Seifert, with an introduction by R. W. Emerson.

82. 1933. Tokyo: Shunsu Bunko. 262 p. Translated into Japanese by Kodate Seitaro.

83. 1934. Tokyo?: Yoshio Shincho Bunko. Translated by Imai. Shincho Library Edition. Sub-edition of 64?

84. 1936.* New York: Grosset and Dunlap. 451 p. The Universal Library Edition.
   This was reissued in 1942 with a jacket bearing the statement that its low price ($1.00) was made possible "by the author's acceptance of a reduced royalty"! A sub-edition of 43.

85. 1936.* Camden, New Jersey: Haddon Craftsmen. 29 p. Illustrated by Richard Ellis. A partial text. Entitled *House-Warming and Winter Visitors from Walden*: *or Life in the Woods*. Privately printed for distribution to friends of the publishers.

86. 1936.* Boston: Printed at the Merrymount Press. xiii, 290 p. With an introduction by Henry Seidel Canby and illustrations by Edward Steichen. Limited to 1500 copies. Limited Editions Club Edition.
   The Monthly Letter of the Limited Editions Club No. 85 (June, 1936) is devoted to a description of this edition.

87. 1937.* Boston: Houghton Mifflin Company. xxiv, 848 p. Introduction, biographical note and annotation by Henry Seidel Canby, illustrated with photographs. Entitled *The Works of Thoreau*. Includes the entire text of *Walden* and selections from Thoreau's other writings. Parent edition of 110.

88. 1937. New York: The Macmillan Company. 391 p. With an introduction by Joseph L. King. A sub-edition of 75.

89. 1937.* New York: The Modern Library. xx, 732 p. Introduction by Brooks Atkinson. Entitled *Walden and Other Writings of Henry David Thoreau.* Includes the entire text of *Walden* and excerpts from most of Thoreau's other works. Modern Library Edition. Parent edition of 125, 121A.

90. 1938.* Chicago: American Technical Society. vi, 218 p. With an introduction and notes by C. B. Cooper.

91. 1938. Washington, D. C.: Library of Congress. 20 12-inch records. Talking Book Edition. Based on the "1929 Macmillan edition" (75).

92. 1938.* Harmondsworth, Middlesex, England: Penguin Books Limited. viii, 278 p. With an introduction by G. B. Harrison and illustrations by Ethelbert White. Penguin Illustrated Classics Edition. Parent edition of 98.

93. 1939.* New York: The Heritage Club. 335 p. Illustrated by Thomas W. Nason. Issued originally for distribution to members of the Heritage Club only, it was later published in an identical edition on the open market.
    The Heritage Club Sandglass No. 7M is devoted to a description of this edition. This issue of the *Sandglass* is also numbered in some copies No. 8B.

94. 1939.* Dunnellen, New Jersey: *The Popular Educator,* I, 40-46. A condensed version.

95. 1940. New York: Thomas Y. Crowell. 423 p. With the biographical sketch by Ralph Waldo Emerson. Entitled *The Works of Henry D. Thoreau.* Includes the entire texts of *Walden, A Week, Cape Cod,* and *The Maine Woods.*

96. 1940.* Pleasantville, New York: *The Reader's Digest,* XXXVII (September, 1940), 129-136. A condensed version.

97. 1942.* New York: W. J. Black, xiv, 358 p. With notes and an introduction by Gordon S. Haight and the biographical sketch by R. W. Emerson. The Classics Club Edition.
    An undated number of *The Classics Club Bulletin* is devoted to a description of this edition.

98. 1942.* New York: Penguin Books, Inc. viii, 278 p. With an introduction [by G. B. Harrison] and illustrations by Ethelbert White. Penguin Book Edition. A sub-edition of 92.

99. 1942. Cleveland: World Publishing Company. iii, 252 p. Illustrated by S. Witkewitz.

100. 1944?* New York: Editions for the Armed Services, Inc. 415 p. Armed Services Edition.
"Overseas edition for the Armed Forces. Distributed by the Special Services Division, A.S.F., for the Army, and by the Bureau of Naval Personnel for the Navy. U.S. Government property. Not for sale."

101. 1944.* Girard, Kansas: Haldeman-Julius Publications. 31 p. With a foreword by Miriam Allen deFord. A condensed version. Entitled *Walden Condensed.*

102. 1944.* Mount Vernon, New York: Peter Pauper Press. 294 p. With illustrations by Aldren Watson.

103. 1945.* Zurich: Artemis-Verlag. xxii, 452 p. Translated into German by Siegfried Lang and with introduction and notes by Fritz Guttinger.

104. 1945.* Buenos Aires: Emece Editores. 329 p. Annotated and translated into Spanish by Julio Molina y Vedia.

105. 1946.* New York: Archway Press. 32 p. Handlettered and illustrated by George Salter. A partial text. Entitled *What I Lived For.*

106. 1946.* New York: Dodd, Mead & Company. xxv, 386 p. With an introduction, interpretive comment and photographs by Edwin Way Teale.
The illustrations in this edition are by far the most helpful group ever gathered together to interpret the text.

107. 1946.* New York: Alfred A. Knopf. x, 169 p. With an introduction by Brooks Atkinson and illustrated with photographs by Henry Bugbee Kane. A series of quotations from *Walden. Entitled Thoreau's Walden*: *A Photographic Register.*

108. 1946.* New York: Modern Library. xxiii, 391 p. With an introduction by Brooks Atkinson (reprinted from the Modern Library Edition of 1937) and illustrations by Charles Locke. Illustrated Modern Library Edition.

109. 1947.* Wien: Amandus-Edition. 40 p. Translated into German and with an afterword by Dr. Augusta V. Bronner. A partial text. Entitled *Einfachheit und höhere Gesetze*.

110. 1947* Boston: Houghton Mifflin Co. xviii, 848 p. Introduction, biographical note and annotation by Henry Seidel Canby. Entitled *The Works of Thoreau*. Includes the entire text of *Walden* and selections from Thoreau's other writings. The Cambridge Edition. A sub-edition of 87.

111. 1947.* Chicago: Packard and Company. xxii, 483 p. With an introduction and bibliography by George F. Whicher. Entitled *Walden and Selected Essays*. Includes *Walden* and six additional essays by Thoreau. University Classics Edition.

112. 1947.* New York: The Viking Press. 696 p. With an introduction and bibliography by Carl Bode. Entitled *The Portable Thoreau*. Includes *Walden* and excerpts from his other works.

113. 1947.* Stockholm: Wahlstrom & Widstrand. 426 p. Translated into Swedish and with an introduction by Frans B. Bengtsson. With illustrations by Stig Asberg.

114. 1948.* Tokyo: Chikushi Shobo. viii, 67, 63 p. Introduced, annotated and translated into Japanese by Toru Okamoto. Contains only "Where I Lived," "Sounds," "Visitors," and "The Ponds," in both Japanese translation and English. Helix Library Edition.

This edition has such delightful annotations as "Sudbury: post village in Massachusetts, on the New York, New Haven and Hartford Rivers" and "Shrub-oak: scrub oak—any of many dwarf American pines."

115. 1948.* Tokyo: Dai-sen Bookstore. 410 p. Translated into Japanese by Emai Kisei.

116. 1948.* New York: Rinehart & Co., Inc. xii, 304 p. With an introduction by Norman Holmes Pearson. Rinehart Edition.

117. 1949.* New York: The Comet Press, Inc. 41 p. With an anonymous foreword and illustrated by Edwin B. Kolsby. A partial text. Entitled *Walden: The Ponds*. Fifteen hundred copies were produced for friends of the publishers.

118. 1949. Leipzig: Dieterich. xviii, 289 p. Translated into German by Anneliese Dangel.

119. 1949.* Buenos Aires: Espasa Calpe Argentina. 298 p. Translated into Spanish and with an introduction and annotation by Justo Garate. Coleccion Austral Edition.

120. 1949.* Kobenhavn: Kunst og Kultur. 401 p. Translated into Danish by Ole Jacobsen, with a foreword by Jacob Paludan, and illustrations by Mads Stage. Entitled *Livit i Skovene*.

121. 1949.*New York: New American Library of World Literature. 221 p. With an anonymous introduction.

Although the copyright page implies that this is a fourth printing of the 1942 Penguin Book Edition (98), it is set up from new plates, with different pagination, and lacks both the illustrations and introduction from the earlier edition.

121A. 1950. New York: Carlton House. 297p.

Reprinted from the plates of the Modern Library Edition, but omits all except *Walden* itself. A sub-edition of 89.

122. 1950.* New York: Doric Books. 303 p. With illustrations by Anthony Saris.

123. 1950.* New York: Harper & Brothers. xii, 440 p. With an introduction by Joseph Wood Krutch. Harper's Modern Classics Edition. A sub-edition of 43.

124. 1950.* Tokyo: Mikasa Shobo. 252 p. Translated into Japanese by Hoitsu Miyanishi. Entitled *Mori No Seikatsu*. Issued in the Sekai Shiso Sensho series.

125. 1950.* New York: The Modern Library. xxiv, 732 p. Introduction by Brooks Atkinson, foreword by Townsend Scudder. Entitled *Walden and Other Writings of Henry David Thoreau.* Includes the entire text of *Walden* and excerpts from most of Thoreau's other works. Modern Library College Edition. A sub-edition of 89.

126. 1950. München: Münchner Buchverl. 15 p. Translated into German by Fritz Krokel. A partial text. Entitled *Wofür ich Lebte.*

127. 1950. Prague:—?—. Translated into Czechoslovakian, and illustrated by Rudolph Ruzicka, with an introduction.

This edition was impounded by the Russians "pending idealogical investigation into its contents." And I have been unable to discover if the edition was ever released for publication.

128. 1951.* New York: W. W. Norton & Co., Inc. 354 p. With an introduction by Basil Willey and illustrations by Henry Bugbee Kane. Parent edition of 129.

129. 1951.* New York: W. W. Norton & Co., Inc. 354 p. With an introduction by Basil Willey and illustrations by Henry Bugbee Kane. An edition limited to 500 sets was issued boxed with parallel editions of *Cape Cod* and *The Maine Woods,* but they are distinguishable from the major edition only by a note on the dust jacket. A sub-edition of 128.

130. 1951. Tokyo: Iwanami Shoten. 2 vol. Translated by Saburo Kanki. Iwanami Bunko edition.

131. 1952. London: Eyre & Spottiswoode. 354 p. Illustrated.

132. 19??. London: Blackie and Son. 4 vol., 60 p., 60 p., 61 p., 54 p. Transcribed into Grade 2 Braille.

The Abernethy Library of Middlebury College has a copy of this edition purchased prior to 1939. Dr. Viola White, the curator there, writes that she is unable to identify it further since it is entirely in Braille. The Library of Congress had a copy but gave it away, and so is now unable to give any further information. Strangely enough the Blackie company has written me that they have no record of ever having published such a book. It is possible that it was published by some organization for the blind, and that either 34 or 65 was used as the basis for the text.

APPENDIX

A. The Manuscript of *Walden*.

The printer's copy of the manuscript of *Walden* has apparently disappeared, but there is in the Huntington Library at San Marino, California (HM 924), a bundle of 628 pages of Thoreau manuscript which has long been recognized as the material from which *Walden* was made. F. B. Sanborn made an ill-fated attempt to edit this material in his 1909 Bibliophile Society edition of *Walden* (42), but the only thorough study of the manuscript was made by Mr. James Lyndon Shanley, who has made a preliminary report on his findings in "A Study of the Making of *Walden*" in *The Huntington Library Quarterly*, XIV (February, 1951), 147-170.

B. The Corrected Proof of the First Edition.

There is also in Huntington Library (HM 925) a set of the corrected proof of *Walden*. There has never been any extended report made on this material.

C. Serialization of *Walden*.

Brief excerpts from *Walden* appeared in *Sartain's Union Magazine*, XI (July and August, 1852). The magazine ceased publication with the August, 1852, number, raising the interesting speculation: Did Thoreau intend serialization of a large part of *Walden?* No collation of these articles with the first edition has ever appeared in print, although it is obvious at a glance that there are many variations in the text. Only one of these however seems of great importance. In the twelfth paragraph of the chapter entitled "Sounds," the book version says, "reminding me of foreign parts," while the serial version says, "reminding me of foreign ports"—which makes more sense and makes it seem likely that the book version is a misprint which not even the author caught (See note under 5).

Index

(Numerals refer to edition numbers)

ADVANCE COPIES HAVE BEEN DISTRIBUTED
WITHOUT CHARGE TO THE MEMBERS OF THE
BIBLIOGRAPHICAL SOCIETY OF THE UNIVERSITY
OF VIRGINIA. IN ADDITION TO THESE ADVANCE
SHEETS, 250 COPIES HAVE BEEN PRINTED AND
BOUND. THESE MAY BE PROCURED FROM THE
UNIVERSITY OF VIRGINIA PRESS, CHARLOTTES-
VILLE, VIRGINIA AT $2.50 PER COPY.

The End